How to Make Fantastic Gift Baskets!

How to Make Fantastic Gift Baskets!

SPECIAL SECRET RESOURCE!

Basket Making - Your Undisputed Resource For Creating Professional Looking Baskets!

Discover How You Can Make Some Of The Best Looking, And Brilliantly Woven Baskets That Would Win The Heart Of Every Other Person Who Takes A Look At It, And Make Them Want To Take One Home With Them...!

At Last! A Power-packed Guide That Would Assist You With Your Newly Found Basket Making Passion, And Will Help You Make Baskets That Look Professional And Catchy! Maybe You Are The Next Basket-making Guru In The Making... !

AVAILABLE ONLY FOR A VERY LIMITED TIME!

Discover the Joys of Basket Weaving! New Hands-On Guide Covers Everything You Need to Know To Become an Expert!

This comprehensive ebook features:

- A general overview of basket making
- Basket weaving terminology
- Differences in basket weaving styles and techniques
- How to make two easy and functional baskets
- A description of common tools and materials needed for basket weaving
- Information about specific textures and weaves used in basket weaving
- Helpful hints and tips
- A metric conversion chart
- A list of basketry associations and guilds
- Numerous photos
- And much more!
- In-depth coverage of the history and geography of baskets
- Detailed advice on basket design, materials, techniques, care, and repair!
- Step-by-step instructions for making an array of baskets!
- And much, much more!

DOWNLOAD NOW

"Sensational Breakthrough Movement Exposes The Revolutionary Ways To Attract And Manifest Anything You Want In Life, Like Magic!"

Long-Kept Secrets Never Before Explained About How To Create The Life Of Your Dreams Finally Revealed In Startling Materials!

HARNESS THE HIDDEN LAWS OF THE UNIVERSE

How to Make Fantastic Gift Baskets!

Contents

Food Gift Baskets: Getting Started

If you are serious about gifting, gift-giving, with quality food-baskets, standard, low-end, even upscale and gourmet food gift baskets, you need to take some time and consider, stop and analyze:

Who will be getting the basket and why, the budget, cost and how much you want to spend on contents, packaging, shipping and handling as all this forms part of the overall expense and process.

Secondly, you need to more closely analyze the nutrient content of food items in a standard to extravagant food gift basket.

Five MORE reasons that food gift baskets do so very well, for so many people, individuals and groups, purposes and goals:

1.   Have a spirit of inquiry, curiosity, excitement and real interest in and about the other person(s) in the process, the recipient. When buying or assembling a food gifts basket(s), you need to listen to and consider other people's interests about your own
2.   You are not giving something to get something in return
3.   The best gift ever, even for food gift baskets are those ones that improve, complement or enrich the overall standing and quality of life, experience or indulgence for someone else.
4.   Gifting is selfless and going beyond, that extra mile for someone else and what it important for them, not buying a gift that you like, or would like to receive.
5.   Focus in on the recipient's preferences and lifestyle. Be genuine and authentic in your giving, not even wanting anything in return, not even a thank you (you will be getting those in abundance anyway without even lifting too much of a finger in the process, your food gift baskets will do the talking and preparation for you! You just sit back and enjoy the spoils.

Food Gift Baskets: A Business On The Rise

Insider sourcing on the topic, show that the markets for these types of food and gourmet gift baskets are growing and continuing the upswing in this section of the marketplace. There are many a good reason for that strong a showing.

1.   A thoughtful, quality, hand-selected, synergized and well-presented gift basket has style, elegance, class, making gifting easy as ever, with wide variety, choice and options across categories, gender, age, types of gifts, budgets even borders.

2.   There are numerous themed Gift Basket for anyone, someone special, everyone and every occasion, event and celebration.

3.   Putting together a quality food gift baskets giving option and perfect gift does not have to complex, back-breaking, pocket-book friendly and take minimal time and effort, energy and input from your end (as much or as little hands-on as you would like to be.

4.   It is a time and money saver that puts you way ahead of the pack.

5.   Size, variety, costs, content all vary and it is an accommodating process and outcome for a diverse set of interest individuals and groups.

6.   Effortless, flexibility, versatility, affordability to name but a few of the stellar reasons to risk and reward yourself and others with putting together the perfect food gift baskets, whether for personal giving, corporate/business, holidays, special occasion etc.

7.   Food gift baskets are the perfect partner even for the budget conscious giver, welcomed by all recipients and pocketbooks alike. You will still receive the recognition for effort, although it took very little. Someone who gets one of these food baskets, will remember and thank you for it.

8.   A variety of smaller items, is both economical, good value and a great gift to give and/or receive.

9.   As a tangible expression of friendship, gratitude, recognition etc. it is and can be truly unique and personal.

10.   Anyone and everyone, somebody and everybody, loves receiving these tokens and edible delights .

Food Gift Baskets are the perfect solutions for everyone who knows someone who is difficult to shop for or who has everything. Handmade food gift baskets carry a nice personal touch that very few can one-up (not that that is what it is all about, but what it does for you, is put you on a higher level of gifting and gift giving, rising above mediocrity.

<u>Food Gift Baskets: Why It Works</u>

Food kits and food gift baskets, sets and boxes all say a lot about sender, recipient, their relationship, the purpose, process and outcome. They all matter! Food basics, kits, cooking solutions, special treats, themed baskets, gourmet, celebration-type baskets, all holidays, occasions, events and special days/people can be celebrated with a thoughtful food gift basket.

These types of specialty gifts and foods type gifting, allow the giver to be creative, expressive, personal, intimate, without affront, risk, combined with assured satisfaction and reward, acceptance and reciprocation, appreciation and such positive, overwhelming responses that gifting will become a no-brainer in no time flat. Food Gift Baskets take your Gift Innovations, Creativity And Customized Giving to a whole new level. This will be the time for you to let your creative, imagination and budget take flight in coming up with great new food gift ideas, not run of the mill, low-end, upscale, extravagant, but personalized and meaningful gifts that speak to the heart of the matter, the recipient! This is the ONE format of giving that is not about you but all about the one receiving the thoughtfully put together, even pre-assemble, package type image. The basket still says: selected, chosen for me, by someone else and I matter! This is great!

It affords choice, variety, options, possibilities and lots of price ranges to choose from. Even themed, personalized, custom-baskets, Organic, Eco-Friendly, Environment-Conscious Giving Options and select, superior and prime gourmet, brand selections of food gift baskets can works its magic for you.

Making choices for other remain hard to do. Tailoring a food gift basket to someone else 's craving, choices and preferences can be hard at first, but you can decipher what it takes rather effortlessly. Consumables, fresh produce, processed foods, snacks, treats, home-made goodies, meat, dairy, sweet, salty, there are numerous options to choose from.

Food Gift Baskets that are wonderfully crafted and assembled as edible tokens of gratitude and recognition, appreciation or special occasion celebration-type giving has never been easier. The most commonplace starting point for discerning shoppers and gift-givers is who it is for, what would be suitable, how much to spend (all included, content, packaging, shipping, handling, delivery, insurance etc.) Staring with a theme and creating a the basket for and around your recipient's needs, preferences and interests can make it easier to get off to a good start. You can spend some time, inquiry and effort trying to find out what they like, listening for cues and clues as to what they prefer, crave and appreciate, are fond of etc. Build and fill the basket according to these principles theme and recipient.

There are so many different types of themes you can start with, that possibilities, promise and potential might overwhelm you, but you can take control of the process, starting with the right container, content, covering or wrapping, decorative touches, personalized note, card and timely delivery. Giving food gift baskets recipients something to be thankful for, is what it is all about.

Food Gift Baskets: Presentation And Delivery

It is not just about what goes into the food gift baskets, but also how you present and deliver it.

Here are some refined touches and final considerations to include in your food gift baskets giving:

-   Is presentation part of the gift, how important are things like covering, wrapped in clear cellophane, see-through type properties or boxed up for surprise element and wow factor for the recipient.?
-   Clear wrap or container, specialty food contents safe and secure?
-   Ribbons, additions and enhancements?
-   Cards or not (documents – import/export, courier, delivery)?
-   Shipping Boxes, packaging and company (reputation, word of mouth, customer testimonials and such favorable, reliable, reputable, affordable)?

-   Protection, replacement insurance, unsolicited package documentation and clear markings (sender/recipient), labels, notes , personalization items, etc.

-   Ensuring your food stuffs, produce and content choices are tasty, tested and specialty item type delicacies is but one step towards perfection. Synergizing everything together into harmonious gift unit gets you closer. Quality, originality and hand-picked customized goods will make your food gift basket valuable and if packaged and shipped well, a guaranteed winner!

 Whether hand-delivery, local, far-way, international, courier, door-to-door, ordering online, in person, DIY (do-it-yourself), snail-mail, gift-cards, electronic redeemable, virtual gift baskets *yes there are those options too!) worldwide, domestic, by air, train/rail, wheel or hand, your food gift baskets can and will arrive safely if you plan, prepare and execute the finer details and not just focus on what goes into it or how much it costs, how to present and/or cover, even beautify it.

Food Gift Baskets: Reasons To Use

Five MORE reasons that food gift baskets do so very well, for so many people, individuals and groups, purposes and goals:

1.   Have a spirit of inquiry, curiosity, excitement and real interest in and about the other person(s) in the process, the recipient. When buying or assembling a food gifts basket(s), you need to listen to and consider other people's interests about your own

2.   You are not giving something to get something in return

3.   The best gift ever, even for food gift baskets are those ones that improve, complement or enrich the overall standing and quality of life, experience or indulgence for someone else.

4.   Gifting is selfless and going beyond, that extra mile for someone else and what it important for them, not buying a gift that you like, or would like to receive.

5.   Focus in on the recipient's preferences and lifestyle Be genuine and authentic in your giving, not even wanting anything in return, not even a thank you (you will be getting those in abundance anyway without even lifting too much of a finger in the process, your food gift baskets will do the talking and preparation for you! You just sit back and enjoy the spoils.

Food Gift Baskets: Why Give One?

Fruits, gourmet foods, edible gifts, chocolates, organic foods, treats and snacks, cookies, sweets and cheese a hallmark gift-giving enterprise in recent years, a growing trend and convenient, affordable way to spoil someone, say thank you, celebrate and share.

You can easily find low-end to higher upscale baskets, beautifully designed for every occasion and special individual that you want to honor by giving a personalized or general food gift basket to. Holiday and corporate gifts lend themselves perfectly to this tradition and channel of giving. Brand names goods, baby baskets with formula, teething biscuits and rice cereal will be welcomed by recipients with open arms, thankful for your thoughtful, practical gift.

A creative expression, indulgent selection synergized and put together with basket, ribbon and bow makes the perfect gift for someone special. You can purchase and order right online or make one yourself. Prices ranges from $50 to hundreds and can even include a gift card to a specialty store or organic food market, local grocer, department store and more. Pasta kits, area-foods, themed baskets, backpacking, country-style, meats and hams, salmon, cooking kits, partnered with wine, cheese servers, trays, woks, cooking utensils, chocolates, even silk scarf and/or gloves, hat, leather folios, all make for some unique gifts.

Why give a food basket? It is versatile, affordable, unique and will be remembered, enjoyed and appreciated by recipients young and old. Seasonal, special holiday celebration food gift baskets, bath and body, baby-kits, children gifts, games, stories, activities, personal care products and more can add to your selection and variety. You can make a lasting impression with a food gift basket.

From premium, upscale to low-end, practical, useful and yummy, there are food gift baskets for every palette and budget available.

Coffee, tee and chocolate food gift baskets are popular, as are cheese, dip and salsa, signature, brand gourmet foods.

Food Gift Baskets: What To Look For In The Finished Product

For choice food gift baskets or gift-items that are fresh produce, seafood, fruits, cheeses (refrigerated products), packaged meats, dairy, melting-possibilities, etc. extra care need to be taken, even beyond putting the items, packaging together into a unit. It has to be safe, not damage in the process, from one point to another point, supplier, shipper, recipient for example!

Guard against and consider things like

- Perishable, non-perishable (expiry dates, food safety, bacteria, exposure sun, light. Other foods (smells, taste etc.)
- Opt for vacuum-sealed, freshness sealed in type packaging, coverings
- Shipping distance, location, timing (how long will take to get there, will it arrive in one piece, mint condition)
- Breakable, fragile (what type of packaging, shipping materials, extra cushioning is used in the process)
- Shelf-life, refrigeration (heating/cooling)
- Restrictions
- Hand- delivery, point-to-point courier, mailing, by air/ground
- Cost
- Signatures
- Insurance
- Getting what you ordered and paid for

Is presentation part of the gift, how important are things like covering, wrapped in clear cellophane, see-through type properties or boxed up for surprise element and wow factor for the recipient.

Clear wrap or container, specialty food contents safe and secure

Ribbons, additions and enhancements

Cards or not (documents – import/export, courier, delivery)

Shipping Boxes, packaging and company (reputation, word of mouth, customer testimonials and such favorable, reliable, reputable, affordable)

Protection, replacement insurance, unsolicited package documentation and clear markings (sender/recipient), labels, notes , personalization items, etc.

Ensuring your food stuffs, produce and content choices are tasty, tested and specialty item type delicacies is but one step towards perfection. Synergizing everything together into harmonious gift unit gets you closer. Quality, originality and hand-picked customized goods will make your food gift basket valuable and if packaged and shipped well, a guaranteed winner!

Whether hand-delivery, local, far-way, international, courier, door-to-door, ordering online, in person, DIY (do-it-yourself), snail-mail, gift-cards, electronic redeemable, virtual gift baskets *yes there are those options too!) worldwide, domestic, by air, train/rail, wheel or hand, your food gift baskets can and will arrive safely if you plan, prepare and execute the finer details and not just focus on what goes into it or how much it costs, how to present and/or cover, even beautify it.

Food Gift Baskets: Eco-Friendly Options

It is not at all hard or challenging to put together an organic, eco-friendly, environment-friendly food gift basket. This could be your contribution to saving the planet, going green(er) and protecting the environment, all in one showing of gratitude, expression or celebration. Recycled or hand-made baskets, paper, wrapping, tissue paper with choice items inside and out, including organic produce, seeds, herbs and flavorings, items and tools for herb gardens, small vegetable plants, planting, composting and/or recycling items can make a statement and spoil the recipient, especially if this is something near and dear to their hearts, convictions and habits. Show your support for them and the environment with a thoughtful gift put together with love and recognition to/for the things that matter to them. You might be surprised by the reaction and extend of the gratitude that you receive.

Putting a food gift basket together using or around central themes will make the process and outcome come together nicely and easily, without too much hassle and complexity, even keeping costs low (if that is a consideration also and budgets somewhat tight). They can also be choice produce, of organic fruit, gourmet, natural foods, vegan, vegetarian or alternative, ethnic, even geographic. Your Food gift basket from and of nature, will and can contain both fresh and processed, pre-packaged, even home-made foods, snacks, coffee and even chocolates. Balance and set the items in the basket, picking fresh ingredients and produce with a long shelf-live and firm texture. Go for variety, selection and top-grade quality fruits, flowers, plants, edible delicacies from the garden, farms and fields.

Veggies, herbal and specialty teas, nuts, snacks, preserves and jams, raw soup mixes, home-made recipes energy bars, wooden cooking utensils and even organic flowers for including in salads and garnish can all be included in this organic field-fest. As to the format and type of basket container, you can let your imagination run wild.

For eco-friendly food gift baskets, you can choose from wood, fiber, straw, woven baskets, hand-made, pottery, tea pots or recycled jars, bowls, clay pots, colander and other objects and items around the house. Raffia adds a nice touch to this orchestra and tribute to nature in a basket.

Food Gift Baskets For Special Occasions

There is probably a basket possibility for every imaginable holiday, special occasion and person on your list, regardless of things like age, gender, affiliation or event.

Here are just some of the trends in modern gifting and gift-customization that have people flocking to food fits baskets options and choices for those special someones and sometimes.

Consumers can make their selection from select, upscale, top-grade, classy, stylish, brand-name, grand, choice Gourmet Gift Baskets, order to have them shipped and delivered anywhere around the globe, with same day shipping available, instant delivery of your greatest gifts, thoughts and edible treats, in one decadent, indulgent, thoughtful food gift basket like no other. There are attractive, individualized options and food gift baskets available from a variety of online and store-front suppliers, main-stream and niche providers alike. Literally thousands of Food Gift Baskets can be assembled, on demand to specification with great savings, birthday greetings, even corporate food baskets and gifting can be easily addressed in no time.

Interesting food gift baskets, themed (sports) or even gourmet popcorn in decorative tins, special occasion, holiday for Christmas, Easter, birthdays food Gift Baskets with the finest ingredients, treats and snacks are great options as edible tokens of love, gratitude, celebration, recognition etc.

Food stuffs, cookies, fruits, wine and cheese, taco, nachos, pasta-kits, salsa and sauces, all can be assembled in real-time as per your selection or purchased, pre-assembled goodies for ease, comfort and scrumptious deliciousness, ribboned and bowed together with attention and ease. These food gift baskets are a hallmark and tell-tale sign of a growing business and trend in gifting and giving around the globe. People have less and less time to shop for individuals and these are a great way to put something special together, without having to the legwork yourself necessarily. For others these will serve as inspiration to let their creativity and wallets go on a wild ride, putting together creatively the perfect selection of food gift baskets for everyone on their gifting list!

Food Gift Baskets: Variety And Choice On Demand

Whether you are on the hunt for the perfect gift, gift basket, gourmet or memory box type Food Gift Baskets, for birthdays as a Thank You , to express sympathy, get well thoughts, Fruit Baskets, romantic indulgent, seductive, erotic/exotic, valentine's treats, Parent-type celebratory gestures for Mother's and/or Father's Day, even Corporate gifting and food Gift Baskets, they are ideal for sharing with anyone at any time of the year. They satisfy and address a variety of budgets and needs.

Whatever your particular event, celebration, Christmas gesture, conference attendee, speaker thank you gift, Even themed giving for Secretaries Day for example, you will find food gift baskets for every occasion, preference, niche and budget.

Celebrating special moments, just got a lot easier with a customized food gift baskets idea for a New Baby, promotion, graduation, housewarming, etc. Cookies, bar-b-q, picnics-to-go-, concert in the park, apples/fruit, chocolates, coffees, teas, wine, popcorn, themed baskets (movies, sports-event, super bowl, golf-tournaments, marathons, etc.), appetizers, cheese and crackers, sweet, savory, seafood, parties in a basket, tastes of Italy, Greece, France etc. Baby Gifts, Birthday Gifts, Culture, area and ethnic traditional cuisine type Baskets for/from areas where people are from, Spa Baskets, Theme Gift Bags & Boxes

Wedding & Anniversary food gift baskets, even Wine Gourmet Gifts will not pose a challenge with all the wide ranges, variety and choice, at your fingertips, to your specification, according to your taste and budget.

The recipient will be sure to be pleased with the quality selection of food gift baskets that givers assemble, order and get on their behalf, left being felt spoilt, appreciated and loved, simply by accepting this token of giving and gifting that goes above and beyond. Price ranges for food gift baskets can be low-end, cost-cutting, effective, budget-conscious, all the way up to essential, affordable, even upscale, extravagance. Food gift baskets priced under $50, to over $100, even $500+ can fit budgets of all sizes and scope and take gifting and giving to a whole new level.

Food Gift Baskets: Coffee, Tea, Chocolates And More

Surprise even those whom you might have a hard time appreciating, surprising themselves, appreciating and just express to your family, friends, guests and others, signaling how special they really are , with just the right food gift basket.

You can assemble a selection of their favorite, seasonal or special fruits, snacks and chocolates for example, for a quite affordable or extravagant gift , pending your preference, budget and recipient reaction that you have in mind! You can awe and wow, you can spoil and have them indulge a little with sweet, savory, salty, delicious and scrumptious feasts in a basket.

They are potable, robust, forgiving, personal, quite effective and even suitable for corporate and business gifting, which has become rife with etiquette, policy and guidelines in recent years. Food gift baskets can make Executive Gifts, Professional Gift Ideas for Clients, Business Associates, Customers, Sales, Marketing and Employee Appreciation a lot easier and simpler to do. Choice produce, products, brands and selections of gourmet food, treats, snacks, chocolate, tea and coffee, by itself, category, combined, themed, teamed up with other things like wines, glasses, cooking utensils, books, pictures, photo-albums, wedding favors, etc. (depending on the occasion and recipient), can make for the perfect and most thoughtful gift, gifting innovation that you can conjure up. You can assemble them from scratch yourself or purchase pre-assembled 'packages; from specialists and mainstream, niche type providers that can take care of all the details, pricing, choice, delivery etc. (even the card!), making it easy one-stop shopping and gifting options for those on the go, with limited (or unlimited) funds and means at their disposal. Regardless of the challenge or the person, there are food gift baskets available for all needs, occasions and everyone, everywhere under the sun.

Exceptional, exotic, fruits, dried assortment (figs, apricots, grapes, apples, teamed up with chocolates and nuts make for great food gift baskets. These gift-units and assemblies even address the needs of allergies, special diets, even cultural giving across borders, made easy and simpler.

Food Gift Baskets: How To Put One Together

So, where to you start? Budget, container, trimmings, content, message, timing, order through payment and delivery and then enjoying it with the recipient basking in the reward of process and outcome. That is it! Plain and simple. Putting together the perfect food gift baskets are not hard at all (neither intended to be). They are meant to make life and gift-giving simpler and easier on all of us.

For example: box, case, crate, basket, woven, wood, plastic, container of what shape, size are to be used, would be a great start. That is part of the basics and fundamentals of what it takes to put together the perfect food gift baskets for others to give and receive, open and enjoy. A pre-packaged or customized, personal, for person type choice gifting for those of discerning, thoughtful giving in mind.

Take the example of food gift baskets that have dried fruits, chocolate covered blueberries and cherries mingled with roasted and salted cashews and pistachios for example. To group them, pick and combine them is half the fun! Then finding the right container to present and display, cover and beautify it with ribbons, bows, lace, plastic, colors and cards are all what the fun and enjoyment is all about when assembling a unique and special food gift basket for someone special.

Savory cheese samplers, food preparation kits with recipe books, Tasty tea-time treats, snacks, cookies, tea and treats, in a tea-pot or cup, with a color satin ribbon, inside a gift picnic basket for example, just keeps on giving, even after the moment of first receiving and opening it. The gift continues to give and give – way after opening and discovering all the treasures inside. Culinary delights and edible treats, home-made goodies and special gourmet, imported goods, ingredients and food-items have long been favorites to give and receive. Now, if its comes together in the perfectly balanced food gift baskets that are available in the marketplace today, all the better to set forth and live on in tradition and minds of others, paying if forward for generations to come, it can only be a good thing to give and to receive!

Food Gift Baskets: Packaging And Delivery

Most of us are so taken in and busy with putting things together or selecting the perfect food gift baskets, that we often overlook, underestimate of forget the most important facts and aspects of this giving gesture and process! No, not what goes into it (well, OK! That too, but from another angle) – taking a practical perspective, over indulgent, extravagant or aesthetically pleasing presentation. Function over beauty is the rule of thumb here if delivery options are complex, far, shipping and delivery will take time or even cross borders, board and airplane, courier service, lots of handling along the way etc. OR even if it is to be hand-delivered.

When you are giving food gifts, consider allergies, mixing perishables with non-perishables, refrigerated items, things that can be mailed or not, (there are some restrictions to be aware of). Also, pay special care to what is in it and how it is packaged, secured for shipping.

Vacuum-sealed, canned, packaged properly, appropriately and completely is important especially for parcels and baskets going far, far away! Also, ensure that there is nothing in there that might compromise the process (it not getting delivered to its end destination for example, due to insufficient paperwork, clearance or unlawful, unspecified items).

Also, look at the expiry date on food stuffs, tins, cans, bottles etc. Ensure that non of the items will/can break (glasses, bottles), or explode under pressure – if they will be transported by air. The most appropriate, safest, padded, protective type packaging, safety more prevalent over beauty and presentation might have you opting for one method and packaging over another, depending on the delivery options and means at your disposal, how far it will travel, custom, import/export guidelines, allowed and non-allowed substances, contents, if sending by mail, courier, across borders for example.

If you are thinking of sending Kosher Gourmet Baskets, meat and diary products, fish and seafood, Upscale gift baskets. Unique, innovative chocolate (it melts you know!)

There are literally hundreds of food gift baskets ideas out there, we just need to keep them practical too. Think shelf-live when you want fresh, tropical, citrus, fruits, or perishable Gourmet Foods gift baskets, items or single items in larger baskets. Ensure they do not spoil or pose a health risk to the ones that receive them. Remember, safety first with food gift baskets.

Food Gift Baskets Made Simple

When you are looking for practical advice on what to include in a food gift basket or gourmet food gift baskets that reflects taste, freshness and thoughtful giving, it could be as easy as going to your nearest local grocer, farmer's market, food stall, organics market of your choice or in your area and selecting two of each of your or the recipient's, family's favorite fruits, like pears apples bananas peach kiwi, grapes, pineapple some plums etc Next, you need to assemble, arrange, put it in a nice basket with or without a handle. Decorating it, by covering it in a nice transparent wrapping, add a splash of color, with ribbon, bow, flowers, stickers etc. will have you making fruits and food gift baskets in no time flat.

You can also buy these or order online, customizing them whichever way you want or choose from pre-assembled, pre-priced baskets already done up for you. Your selection of the perfect food gifts baskets can also include wines, sherry, juices, utensils, recipe books, pampering products, cheeses with biscuits. Let your imagination take flight for some food gift baskets that no one else has thought of before, for a romantic evening, picnic under the stars, even after dinner baskets, breakfast, brunch or English high-tea, Italian, French, Greek or A LA FAMILY FAVORITE type ingredients, products, spices, accessories, treats and the like for the perfect gift! Here are some more practical thoughts from some creative basket-hopefuls and wanna-be experts.

For a pasta basket, choose tri-color pasta, garlic, pasta sauce, black olives, loaf of Italian bread or biscotti, canned clams, mozzarella cheese, bottle of chianti - and make a red, white & green theme, with ribbons, include a pasta-holder as a gift (for spaghetti) or put it in a stainless colander for that personal flair and statement and perfect kitchen accessory to top off the gift.

For something unique, try a home-made gourmet food basket!!! Like your own signature pancake or scone, muffin mix with jams, syrup and toppings.

Food Gift Baskets: Why Give Them?

When it comes to food gift baskets and giving, there are many reasons we opt so freely to give and receive them – here are some of the top reasons people say they like to use food gift baskets, gourmet food gifts and packages for/as gifts:

- Affordability
- Versatility
- Variety and Choice, Wide selection and price ranges
- Flexible (shipping, delivery)
- Personal, Unique and Individual
- Customizable – a chance for your own personal tastes (or those of your recipient(s) to be recognized and put to work!)
- Ease and convenience - able to give more, quicker and even have someone else take care of it for you

As to what types of containers to use for food gift baskets and related giving, you can be very creative and choose any type of shape, size, color, material that you can find, just ensure that you will be able to fill it, balance and cover it properly to showcase your gift-box content as best you can. It can be functional, but also be part of the gift none-the-less for after-gift enjoyment practicality and use. Bassinet Basket

Woods like, Oak and Black Willow, wicker are very popular
Shapes like Rectangles. Squares, totes, baskets, small, medium and large, antiqued, cloth-lined, even galvanized Buckets with Gold Trim, hand-woven, with/without handle, gold or white even gift boxes, vases, flower-boxes, pots, even cutting boards and trays, kitchen bowls, colanders can all be used for the 'base' or basis, packaging for your food gift baskets – another great avenue for your creativity.

Cookie tins, gift sets, unique containers and any functional object can be used for the basis/basics, foundation or packaging for your food gift baskets, even serving dishes, bowls, laundry baskets, sushi trays, cedar planks, metal baskets (painted), ice buckets, totes, wine-holders, DVD-cases or planters, bamboo steamers, urns, travel trunks or cosmetic cases or wagons – the options and choices, possibilities are truly endless. The creative practical answers are all up to you, your imagination and budget! it may be stylish, elegant, upscale to add value to your gift, or simple, basic, if not unusual, recycled even to fit your budget and pocketbook, Unique and colorful, with character or function before beauty, whichever principle you prefer for your selection, combination and styling – everything will and can go, depending on the occasion, purpose and recipient of course!

Download 100+ Books
Completely Free!
No Hassles...
No Charges...
Just Click And Download
100% Free!
CLICK HERE

This Product Is Brought To You By

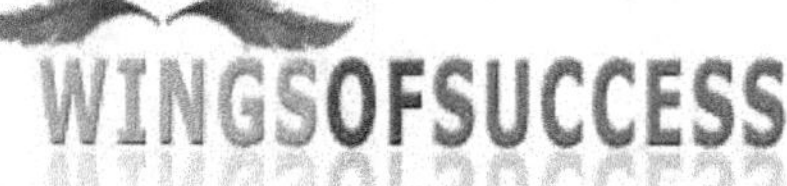